DUPLICITOUS MINDSETS

DUPLICITOUS MINDSETS

A Political and Social Analysis of One Equation . . .

YOSIEF TEWOLDE (SEBER)

To order additional copies of this book, contact:
Xlibris
800-056-3182
www.Xlibrispublishing.co.uk
Orders@Xlibrispublishing.co.uk
787466

Blog https://SeberAngle.wordpress.com
Twitter @Ucf_Seber
Disqus SeberAngle
Facebook SeberAngle
Email SeberAngle@Gmail.com

CONTENTS

PREFACE

In this book, *Duplicitous Mindsets*, I express my other angle—the political angle. I will be deciphering the equation *failure + excuse = blame*.

Acceptance of realities. As stated in my previous book relating to my second-life circumstances, *Glance at Eternity*, acceptance of one's realities is the basis for positive changes where necessary. The results abound to having peace in one's heart. This enables one to encounter progress in one's life. That is the aim and what is searched for by humans in their lifetimes naturally.

The book, in short, will analyse where people fail. They will look for excuses to blame anything to others.

In defining the equation stated above, *failure + excuse = blame*, it seems to me the human nature tends to look outwards rather than look inwards for answers of any nature. Taking the seemingly unchallenging route, one will look for an excuse when one fails. One fails and one finds excuse and, ultimately, one deliberates blame.

I am often labelled as being philosophical, and my view is in this book.

I strongly recommend reading this book in conjunction with my Twitter account. You will find the username in the second page of the book. Furthermore, searching my name in Google.com will give you extensive results related to me.

You will find selected topics below to analyse the stated equation. Let's ride on.

DICTATORS AND TYRANTS

Let us start with the reality that our world today still has a few self-advantageous and self-servient dictators and tyrants who rule by fist and rule by fear rather than rule by hope, which is what is needed and expected by humans. One will find that these entities lack peace in themselves, which is developed from making communication with the self. Unhappy in their hearts, they don't communicate with their hearts and minds, I conclude.

A dictator is outward looking, a ruler with total power over a country and over people, typically one who has obtained control by force or manipulation. A tyrant, likewise, is a cruel and oppressive ruler. Here, I don't intend to list countries ruled by dictators and tyrants today.

First, allow me to define what I believe democracy is and what it entails. In my description, democracy is a process by which people get the opportunity to use their God-given minds and brains to think. Being able to think results in working out development, progress, achievement, be them material. Those who think rightly are then classed as successful, and those who don't are classed unsuccessful. In this case, being unsuccessful is failure—an element of the equation we are analysing.

Let me digress and say, it is one thing that our world seems to be progressing in practising democratic systems and rules in some; on the other hand, the rise of the far right entities is daunting. Sadly, this is not to forget the few remaining elements ruling by dictatorship and tyranny in the unsuccessful countries, as well as those with far right perspectives in traditionally democratic countries.

Going back to the topic, I tend to categorise dictators and tyrants in two aspects.

One set will deny people freedom to speak, freedom to express, freedom to choose, and even freedom to live. Whilst the other worse entities of dictators and tyrants will deny people the opportunity to think. I go 'Hmm . . .'.

The first category of dictators and tyrants who deny people livelihood will seem like angels in comparison to the second category of dictators and tyrants who will deny people to even think. Looking back at countries that are ruled by one of the two above-stated categories, we can see that they are not materially successful or mentally at peace. And that should not come as a surprise.

First and foremost, let me dwell at the conclusive view that I espouse as I share on my Twitter account, stating,

'All #Dictators and #Tyrants claim to be either #Socialist or #Communist in perspectives. Is this a weakness of the #Socialism #Communism scenarios? That is the insidious challenge.' They are entities who are unhappy with themselves, individuals with no peace to share. They will preach that they want to install, for example, self-reliance. You may have heard that a lot from certain elements. How self-reliance can be instated without people having the opportunity to think and look forward is well beyond me. As I said earlier, freedom to think results in working out development, progress, achievement, and more positive routes to success.

Let me briefly talk about communism, socialism espoused in dictators and tyrants, and also a look at capitalism.

Communism and socialism and, similarly, capitalism are economic and political structures. Communism and socialism are meant to promote equality and remove social classes. Whereas, it can be said that capitalism is a system in which a country's trade and industry are controlled by private owners for profit rather than by the state.

In a communist society, ideally, the working class owns everything, and everyone works towards the same communal goal. There are no wealthy or poor people. All are meant to be equal—in my view, equal in disheartenment. Where this description played and produced the statement in real terms is beyond question. In other words, I say, tell me which country achieved success and progress by the process of socialism or communism. Success suggests both heartfelt peace and material indulgence.

In words, communism is a need-based distribution system. Hence, people are not expected to work more than the requirement. As per this, communism results in low production—the results being mass poverty and limited advancements. Socialism's main focus is on equality whilst resulting to negative achievements. Workers earn wages they can spend as they choose, whilst the government, not citizens, owns and operates the means for production.

Capitalism, on the other hand, delivers the practice and package of democracy, allowing people to think, work, and earn to their limits and beyond. The capacity to choose is the main element of focus.

It is important to note that there are elements where countries under capitalism accept and exercise—elements which communism and socialism claim to espouse. For example, the United Kingdom, where I live, provides basic needs, like healthcare, to everyone regardless of their time or effort at work. In the United States of America, welfare and the public education system are a form of socialism. These processes are common in Western democracies in general, being capitalist entities. The more important case is the element of *choice*.

Both communism and socialism are meant to be the opposite of capitalism, where limitations don't exist and rewards come to those who go beyond the minimum. In capitalist societies, owners are allowed to keep the excess production they earn, and competition occurs naturally, which fosters advancement. Capitalism tends to create a sharp divide between the wealthiest citizens and the poorest; however, the wealthiest own the majority of the nation's resources.

An important element to take note at this juncture is, the poor masses will have the opportunity to use the resources the capitalist entities generated, and the masses will have things to look forward to, not necessarily created from a holy or blessed heart of the capitalist element.

However, it is very important to make a solid note that capitalism is guided by the systems and laws enshrined by the constitution based on democracy, whereas in socialism and communism, it boils down to the will of the dictator or tyrant. Their influence, in some places, is as big as not having a constitution in the first place.

Excuses or justifications are used by dictators and tyrants—socialists and communists as they are. Adding to that, they deny livelihoods to the masses so that they concentrate on their basic daily life requirements. In one country, for example, people are denied access to water or electricity, only for the people to be joyous when the water truck comes by and the electricity working, as per the tyrant government wanted. The masses have children in the government working for free. Then the masses will be engrossed in depending on how they will get basic resources, progressing their daily life circumstances, forgetting that they don't have the freedom of mind to think outside having basic resources. They think there may be something called choice, freedom of mind, and the naturally resulting progress encompassing mental, physical, and material indulgences.

Furthermore, currently we see a lot of young people running away from Eritrea, trying to reach the capitalist countries. In my investigation, these would be the young who were born after the independence of Eritrea from Ethiopia, or they would have been something like six or seven years old when Eritrea became an independent country. What these young people grew up with and what they knew in their lives and existence is that Eritrea has many enemies, and through the endless military service they are obliged to undertake, all they came to know is to kill and that they are surrounded by enemies. Their mindset overwhelmed with hate perpetrated by inner fear. Their capacity to think clearly is abrogated.

I hear the communities that emigrated from Eritrea before, when it was a province of Ethiopia, complain that the young who emigrate now only ask for money; they don't aim to manage and progress their life, unlike the generation that emigrated when Eritrea was part of the province of Ethiopia. They don't aim or support their families who live in Eritrea. These are seriously claimed complaints.

The mind manipulation exercised by the dictator or tyrant is evident by the next example. With blocked minds occupied by basic living conditions, it is not a hidden story that the young go even through death with the only purpose of reaching the capitalist democratic nations that espouse development and peace.

The important thing to note here is that an animal would not go towards a scenario where it may die but attack or run away based on its ability. Simultaneously, those humans running away from tyranny even choose to go to death with the only aim to reach capitalist and democratic nations. They don't bother to even die on the way.

One also notices that when those running away from tyranny once make it into the capitalist states, they will not look to develop their livelihoods. To some extent, they even get manipulated by the representatives of the tyrant system from where they fled in the capitalist world. Mind-boggling as this may be, the reality is evidently in play.

On the other hand, to deny space to the learned or better-off people or elements, justifications for the tyranny installed include sayings like 'We are at war' by creating conflicts with neighbours and 'We are sanctioned by the Western democracies', referring to sanctions that came out due to their modus operandi, concluding more or less that the whole world is against them. Talk about any country in those categories, and one will find the same or similar excuses. Blame is the final target. The equation in play here is failure + excuse = blame.

The countries we are talking about are total failures; they will create circumstances that would serve as excuses to go forth and, of course, generate blame to the other parties.

I conclude by stating again that countries ruled by socialism or communism have not proved successful and peaceful in their make-up. People like me who run away from dictatorial or countries with tyranny supposedly ruled by socialism or communism do not tend to run to countries ruled by socialism or communism but to capitalist countries that have freedom and, as a result, successful economies.

Let me underline this fact as I claim on Twitter. All dictators and tyrants, primarily men, claim that they are either socialist or communist in their political outlook, and this is the insidious challenge.

All tyrants avidly complain about the influences from the democratic Western countries, capitalist in their make-up.

Again, how about dictatorships? Briefly speaking, dictators or tyrant rulers are realities that override the ethics of democracy. As stated, democracy, in my view, is a circumstance that gives freedom of mind to think and exercise livelihood by choice and rules by hope, whilst, I say, dictatorship rules by fear. In certain parts of the world, dictators, in my opinion, fall on the same category of unhappy, discontented, calamitous, disgruntled elements. They rule by fear and look for others to blame, and in dictatorships, the easier targets happen to be ultimately the innocent, unsuccessful, poor, and afraid public.

Of course, in dictatorships, one will notice the ruler to be praised to the extent of being like a god by their confused supporters.

To the question, why do the countries ruled by dictatorship and tyranny or socialists or communists seem peaceful? my answer is that it is not that they are ruled by hope and by choice of the people given freedom but that they ruled by fear. Their mindset is blocked, and they are engaged in basic daily life circumstances. There is not mind state that can analyse and act. One does not see demonstrations or walkouts.

As is the case, there are countries that blame culpability, the lack of their successes on other countries and components, without end. Their successful manipulation is sedated and measured by their continual negative rule by fear as opposed to the positive rule by hope which results to development and progress, thereby exercising the freedom of mind for them to exploit.

On the main note, in my view, all dictators claim to be either a socialist or a communist in their political stands, this scenario ruining the positively meant systems of socialism and communism in their context exploited, which, coming from a positive angle, would have a positive effect.

A perfect example of the scenarios described above is the country that will be mentioned below. Let me state what I said on Twitter, '#Eritrea's current negative status is not only the result of #Tyranny and #Dictatorship, BUT also the weaknesses and defaults of the negatively established & biased floundering oppositions, entities who did not even convince me despite my views on dictatorships and tyrannical rules. Mostly established from anger and generally, hate.'

Personally, I never found them fit for the management of the country. To some extent, they can only prove to be worse than the current state of tyranny the country is under. The only point where the lists of oppositions agree on being the hate of the self-nominated president of current Eritrea.

I even come along to say, 'If #Eritrea cannot provide its people—freedom of mind to think exercised by #Democracy and laws & systems exercised by #Constitution—it may as well return a part of #Ethiopia. Those who died for independence died for freedom to think.' One needs to remember that Eritrea had been a province of Ethiopia when it claimed its independence around 1991 (Gregorian calendar).

With the country under negative perspectives from both angles, it should not be difficult to imagine its very low existence. Would anyone choose to live there?

Let us look at the equation failure + excuse = blame in this regard. When a state fails, everyone involved comes up with the phrase 'It is because . . .'. The tyrant claims it is because we are at war and we are sanctioned, for example. The oppositions will also claim because it is a dictatorship. One cannot miss whom to blame. And in many cases, it is the whole world to blame one way or the other.

Allow me to repeat this: I strongly believe that the rudimentary greatness, strength, and power of an entity are determined by whether they rule by hope or they rule by fear.

TALK ABOUT CRIME

The joy of being happy and at peace within the self is lost, and the innovation is taking out one's anger and disheartenment. One example is crime.

Looking at criminal acts, as I write this, I hear and notice that there are high occurrences of stabbings, shootings, and drug-related issues emerging in England, where I live, and similarly in other parts of the world. I feel and understand the assailants, the perpetrators, or the culprits who started the dispute and the victims who are exposed to it. Many are at fault or are weak by different measures. Whilst remembering our equation, failure + excuse = blame, let me state first that it must be underlined that both sides are responsible to different extents. Allow me to explain why I claim both sides are probably at fault.

First, what are the assailants or culprits responsible for? To answer this question, let me direct you to my view on self-management that leads to being happy and contented within oneself, being at peace with the self, and being ultimately successful.

In my definition, in life, happiness comes from self-management and accepting self-circumstances. Let me state what I claim on Twitter, 'Happiness comes from being at peace with the self, Being at peace comes from being positive at the self and being positive comes from Accepting ones conditions.' Personally, I am coming from a state of condition that made me disabled and curtailed my abilities immensely. You may check the book *Glance at Eternity*. Being in my current peaceful mind state, I thank God for enabling me to express myself, having come from a state of having to learn again my name.

Let's go back to the topic at hand. The assailants are those elements that would have failed in a material life and are unhappy within themselves spiritually. Looking at our equation, failure + excuse = blame, human nature tends to look for excuses to find itself surrounded by faults and weaknesses. Despite this, the lack of listening to the self does not provide them with the opportunity to think clearly and accept their weaknesses and faults where necessary, enabling them to focus, change, or address matters in acceptable ways as there is no communication with the self—a very important element. They don't explore the need to either change or avoid the circumstance, following excuses, as their primary aim is to find another one to blame and load off their frustration on others. Calm and open self-diagnosis would have required them to genuinely listen to their minds and hearts calmly and in peace, which will give them the platform for acceptance and to undertake necessary change going towards progress to a positive self-managed life and, ultimately, a happy self with a peaceful mind.

Second, what are the victims or recipient casualties—the ones who get stabbed—responsible for? Let me stress that I don't mean all but many victims. Simultaneously, the recipient elements may have, in some way, failed in life and are unhappy in themselves in many cases. Primarily, they don't listen to themselves; the lack of observation and noticing does not give them the opportunity to avoid or take necessary measures to respond as well as dissociate from assailants as maybe necessary. These entities, too, failed to listen to their hearts and minds in some ways. The results are victims falling to the culprits. Calm, open self-diagnosis would require them to listen to their minds, instincts, and hearts calmly and in peace. By observing to avoid circumstances and respond accordingly, it may well be to run away. Otherwise, what is the point after the damage is done? Failure + excuse = blame. I accept the equation does not play well in this particular title to apply to victims, but I see it as this short scenario. Failing to observe registers as the excuse, not that one failed to observe, but blaming. 'It was not my fault' is the resting ground.

At the third place, where I had been a patient and where I do my voluntary work now, a mental health hospital, directing people in the hospital from the entrance security area, this man came near me and first he said, 'What are you doing here?'

I responded by saying, 'I work here as a volunteer.'

He told me, 'Go away.' He followed me and hurled words like, 'I will bang you cripple out to the street.'

Later I understood that the security people were attending to situations around the hospital, and the office was only manned by one person alone. As I made my way and walked out the gate to avoid any conflict, I saw a lady to whom I mentioned to tell the security that I was being harassed. Furthermore, I came across two workers who asked me, 'What is happening?'

I said, 'I am being harassed.' They told me to come back with them. They managed to calm the person—or, rather, the person realised he couldn't continue his aggression—and reported it to the lady at the security desk. We came to the conclusion that I would go to the library of the hospital for safety. Had I responded to the man, can you imagine what consequences would have transpired, by no fault of mine? I was told by the lady who accompanied me to safety that I dealt with the matter well. Most importantly, I am safe and not angry with the person. I understand measures have been taken in the hospital to transfer the harassing patient elsewhere.

DEMOGRAPHY PERSPECTIVES

I notice a certain demography in England, for example, complaining that they feel targeted by the establishment—the police—based on the rules such as 'stop and search'. It is important to note that this has something to do with the rise in stabbings and violence, majority of which are by young black entities. Therefore, it is only logical and right that more attention is given to the particular demography. Hence, many young black people are stopped and searched.

In summary, under the practice of democracy, the rules that arise as a result of the particular demography that became the assailants or culprits call to the establishment of certain rules such as that stated above—'stop and search'. In my view, the targeted demography that falls under that banner should accept the fact of realities and not conflate them. As the realities encompass, authorities are not going to concentrate and look for 'older white women' to stop and search. Need I say more?

Let's look back at the equation failure + excuse = blame. Those with criminal intent fail themselves. Then according to our equation, they will excuse themselves by suggesting the authorities or police are racist and are working against them. They conclude that the establishment is racist and is avidly to blame for the occurrences, forgetting the realities that a particular demography is in play in these circumstances.

Very important, when I make the above statements, I am reflecting only to standard-minded adults. The statements I am making do not reflect, for example, to young children, mentally handicapped persons, and the like.

Allow me to add one important statement that will be extensively covered in the next title. Imagine a black child growing up listening to statements like 'The authorities are racist' by any failed parent or community leader. That child will not grow up with the ambition to achieve any positive circumstances. 'I have no job because . . .' 'I have no livelihood because . . .' 'I have no peaceful family because . . .' The list is endless.

COMPOSING RACISM

Let me make America as an example in this case. America is wholly a state of immigrants, whether they are of black or white ethnic groups or of other colour. It is interesting to note if asked 'Where are you from?' that black people in America will distance themselves from claiming just American. Instead, they will proudly claim they are African–American. One need not ask further to explore the reply that they were enslaved and suffered from racism. Whilst the white elements will say they are proudly just American, where necessary, they only further explain or detail that their background is British–American or else.

Let me start by introducing what African–American entails in America—a true historic perspective. It is despite that that I will claim accepting self-realities is the foremost matter to be realised.

African–Americans (also referred to as black Americans or Afro–Americans) are an ethnic group of Americans with total or partial ancestry from any of the black racial groups of Africa. The term typically refers to descendants of enslaved black people who are from the United States. As a compound adjective, the term is usually punctuated as *African–American*.

Blacks and African–Americans constitute the third largest racial and ethnic group in the United States (after white Americans and Hispanic and Latino Americans). Most African–Americans are descendants of enslaved people within the boundaries of the present United States. On average, African–Americans are of West/Central African and European descent, and some also have Native American ancestry. According to the US Census Bureau data, African immigrants generally do not self-identify as African–American. The overwhelming majority of African immigrants identify instead with their own respective ethnicities (~95%). Immigrants from some Caribbean, Central American, and South American nations and their descendants may or may not also self-identify with the term.

Just digressing: Although I have ancestry coming from an African country as a refugee to England, if asked, 'Where are you from?' I insist that I am English or British based on where I chose to reside and where I was accepted as a citizen, unless I was specifically asked where I was born, in which case, a different answer comes describing my history. I have come across people not accepting my responses and perspectives. You have guessed it right. These are people of black or foreign origins, also white English that would have thought, *He can only feel answering as is the norm. I am African.*

African–American history starts in the sixteenth century with people from West Africa forcibly taken as slaves to Spanish America and in the seventeenth century with West African slaves taken to English colonies in North America. After the founding of the United States, black people continued to be enslaved, and the last four million black slaves were only liberated after the Civil War in 1865. Due to notions of white supremacy, they were treated as second-class citizens. The Naturalization Act of 1790 limited US citizenship to whites only, and only white men of property could vote. These circumstances were changed by Reconstruction—the development of the black community, the participation in the great military conflicts of the United States, the elimination of racial segregation, and the civil rights movement which sought political and social freedom. In 2008, Barack Obama became the first black American—or to satisfy certain readers, African–American—to be elected president of the United States.

That being the true history, I say it is very important for it not to be used as an excuse for not managing one's life positively.

Let me continue introducing what white American basically identifies proudly as just American entails.

White Americans are Americans who are descendants from any of the white racial groups of Europe, the Middle East, and North Africa or, in census statistics, those who self-report as white based on having majority-white ancestry.

White Americans (including white Hispanics) constitute the historical and current majority of the people living in the United States, with 72% of the population in the 2010 United States census. Non-Hispanic whites totalled about 197,285,202 or 60% of the US population. European–Americans are the largest ethnic group of white Americans and constitute the historical population of the United States since the nation's founding.

The United States Census Bureau defines white people as those 'having origins in any of the original people of Europe, the Middle East, or North Africa'. Like all official US racial categories, *white* has a 'not Hispanic or Latino' and a 'Hispanic or Latino' component, the latter consisting mostly of white Mexican–Americans and white Cuban–Americans. The term *Caucasian* is synonymous with *white*, although the latter is sometimes used to denote skin tone instead of race. The inclusion of non-Europeans in the definition of *white* is controversial. Many of the non-European ethnic groups classified as white by the US census—such as Arab–Americans, Jewish–Americans, and Hispanics or Latinos—may not be identified as or may not be perceived as white.

The largest ancestries of American whites are German–Americans (17%), Irish–Americans (12%), English–Americans (9%), Italian–Americans (6%), French–Americans (4%), Polish–Americans (3%), Scottish–Americans (3%), Scotch–Irish–Americans (2%), Dutch–Americans (2%), Norwegian–Americans (2%), and Swedish–Americans (1%). However, the English–Americans and British–Americans demography is considered a serious undercount as the stock tends to self-report and identify as simply Americans (7%) due to the length of time they have inhabited the United States, particularly if their family arrived prior to the American Revolution. The vast majority of white Americans also have ancestry from multiple countries.

I sense the above historic description is aimed at addressing what people might respond to my views in the book. To those who want to underscore the history lesson, I say go back and read the book from the beginning and reflect.

Having explored the two perspectives of Americanism, let me continue to talk about the lifetime achievements and progresses. As per the humanly description, let me state achievements and progresses are based on accessing and having more of material and resources.

That raises the important question, do the so self-defined blacks or African–American entities had or have any achievements or progresses? The answer to that is a resounding *no*, except for a few who would have accepted themselves.

Let's address our equation failure + excuse = blame. If you will ask blacks or African–Americans, as they choose to be labelled as such, they will immediately come up with answers like they had been enslaved to date. One will say the reason I do not have a successful career angle is the fact that there is racism against blacks or African–Americans, that the white elements have denied me access. The reason I don't have a peaceful family life is because the whites have denied me whatever it may be. The reason I have failed is because the whites have not treated me well. The course of thinking goes on as such.

Now imagine a black child growing up repeatedly hearing the statements above with the expression of anger. The child growing up with such a negative mindset will not endeavour to achieve and use the God-given brain and instinct, hence only left with the results to fail. Let me also state that my Catholic religious belief does not allow me to think that God may have created the white with a better brain than the blacks. So any success is a result of self-acceptance in my view.

That being so, why are the black-dominated areas of the world in Africa, in Latin America, and so forth still backward and unsuccessful? Because they were all created with the same brain and mind as we said.

Failure + Excuse = Blame

Coming back to my arguments, I see that the failings of black entities, which we see a lot around, will come up with excuses as we saw above—'It is racism that blocked me to success,' for example. Following this route of thinking, the whites are to blame. Again, imagine one growing up with this mantra; the motivation to achieve and progress is curtailed. Then one would get into criminal aspects and relieve the anger built inside to another. Where there are laws and systems, one would end up in prison or be segregated in life.

I don't forget that there may be white entities taking negative advantage of these perspectives. Thinking the right ways would give the right way to address and respond to the issue. The manipulation and misappropriation by the white elements are covered under the title 'Far Right Politics' below. But remember, the white elements take cue from the perspectives of the negative black elements.

As I write this, there are engrossed stabbings taking place in England, predominantly by black entities. I talked about this above. Let us remember, failure + excuse = blame.

FAR RIGHT POLITICS

Primarily, it is right to note far right elements are entities predominantly in capitalist countries. The far right view is an influence directed to the entities and individuals or communities that are unsuccessful and unhappy with themselves, mainly in the capitalist systems, a white perspective. Right-wing populism is in play. If we take our equation again, in today's world, the politics of the far right groups is mainly based on blaming immigrants. They tend to preach to the white people who are engrossed by the thought, downtrodden, unsuccessful, and unhappy with themselves. If you don't have a partner, blame the immigrants. If you don't have a job, blame the immigrants. In conclusion, for all your ills, blame the immigrants.

Failure + excuse = blame—this equation will apply to these groups in that it claims that if you are unsuccessful or you find yourself as a failure, your excuse would be that immigrants have taken over you. And voila, you have something to ascertain your blame to. Furthermore, the political elite are to be blamed for not sending away the immigrants or closing the doors for the immigrants. The weaker elements will be engrossed by anger, and their anger are being taken advantage of by the far right political ideologies, right-wing populists—a rich ground for the far right unholy politics.

As I write this book, the rise of the far right political views seems to be taking its toll. Talking about their influences in Europe, in Western capitalist states, the far right entities access the weak, unsuccessful, dispirited white people, individuals, and communities. Again, the equation I came up with before will rightly apply to these scenarios—failure + excuse = blame. You don't have a family, blame the immigrants. You don't have a job, blame the immigrants. You don't have this, blame the immigrants. You don't have that, blame the immigrants. And so the rhythm plays. Reflection in the self is not there.

Many countries in Europe—like Austria, Italy, taking note of them being capitalists in their political stands—are ruled by the far right elements today and a few in coalitions with the far right parties termed as right-wing populists. On the other hand, some countries like the United States of America, like United Kingdom, and like France, came up with entities that disabled the far right populists from coming into power.

America came up with Donald Trump, Great Britain came up with a party called UKIP, and France came up with an independent Emmanuel Macron. Germany does not currently have a stable government simply because the ruling party did not want to make coalition with the far-right that had gained many winning vote, surviving by coalitions with smaller entities. In particular, UKIP in the UK and Donald Trump in the US in their campaigns and later are heard yet again talking about immigrants and about ways to close borders, even building walls in borders in Donald Trump's case. What they did is they claimed the votes that would have otherwise gone to the far right groups. In France, for example, it is important to note that the far right came close to second to the independent person who finally won despite the older traditional parties being put in the back.

To take note, in my view, it is not the personal perspective or interest for Donald Trump in America and UKIP in the UK to talk extensively about immigrants but it is aimed to impress the public that would have otherwise voted for the far right entities. It's the reason I call them a blessing in disguise on Twitter.

In summary, on far right-wing politics, as I write this, the emergence of far right elements in countries which were ruled by democracy as we know it, mainly in the Western capitalist world, is rising. Far right entities, like dictators and criminals, find entities to blame for their lack of success in their life and happiness and peace within themselves. They target people who are not happy in themselves due to the material paucity, mainly a result of mental deficiency. One good example of this is the blame that the disheartened people's lack of success in life is due to the immigrants, about which we hear a lot in current times—both from the far right wing and those attempting to claim their political territories.

RELIGION IN PLAY

Let us see the equation in terms of religions. It is sad to see circumstances manipulated by religions fall in this category of things—for example, terrorism advocated as a reaction to the so-called Western democracies' successes and practices and the related religious beliefs.

Let's define the equation failure + excuse = blame. People not looking within themselves, noticing unacceptable outcomes, find themselves failing in achieving peace and harmony within themselves, affecting the communities. Failure in play and justification by way of excuses are implied to the free-minded parts of the world. Then blame is deliberated. As mentioned above, terrorism being a perfect part of blame is a negative action. I will not be surprised that in the future, the religion I have in mind may be demised and become history.

In conclusion, for religions that have not been able to induce peace and happiness in the hearts of their followers, their successes become very limited and not satisfactory. Failing to see peace and progress in the particular religion drives making excuses that democratic countries and other religions are making it. Finally, justifying and blaming those entities in different ways become the way—for example, terrorism. Looking within becomes a challenge. Failure + excuse = blame.

INCREMENTAL DEMOCRACY

Let's introduce the element of incremental democracy.

Let me start by defining what I mean by the new term *incremental democracy*. Incremental democracy, in my view, is the establishment of democracy in small steps or little by little for people to grow up with or develop their mindset of the circumstances unfolding in the process.

Taking the examples in history, let me share what transpired when Hitler of Germany came to power, which was a result of an election process. One needs to remember that elections are practices resulting from the practice of democracy.

Also, the Muslim Brotherhood that came to power in Egypt practised democracy as we know it and exercised election, only to win and take power.

However, it needs to be remembered that Hitler in his rule and the Muslim Brotherhood of Egypt had negative agendas on their backs. Their procedural elections were practised, and people did not get the opportunity to investigate their back agendas.

Now we know their negative perspectives when people then did not realise.

It is with this view that I come up with the term *incremental democracy*. If practised, people would have had the opportunity to measure and analyse the perspectives of the entities introducing elections, which are practices of democracy.

ABOUT THE AUTHOR

Born on 5 April 1964 in today's Eritrea, situated in North-East Africa, Yosief Tewolde Zerezghi is a son of a self-employed construction truck driver, the late Tewolde Zerezghi, and a housewife, the late Roshan Ekub, to whom he is writing a book titled *Undimmed Light Mother*. Yosief has one brother, who died in the war between Eritrea and Ethiopia. His feeling about the war makes him say his brother died rather than martyred. He also has three elder sisters.

Yosief studied primary school at Saint Joseph's in Keren and secondary school in the capital city Asmara in a seminary in today's Eritrea.

He joined a religious organisation called Christian Brothers, where he continued following his secondary school. When he reached the working age, he was assigned by the organisation to attend his career training in Ethiopia. Subsequently, he was assigned to teach in Eritrea and Ethiopia.

Considering the bad political situation under Ethiopia, he moved to England, the United Kingdom, in 1989 as a refugee fleeing the conflict that was taking place in Eritrea and the unacceptable political manoeuvres. He went to university and achieved a degree in chemical engineering and a master's degree in environmental science. Yosief worked in various organisations as a process engineer and safety engineer.

Yosief had an active life that went bizarrely to a different direction, following a drastic accident which he chooses to claim as an incident that involved a train. The major results of the situation were brain damage, amputation, and blindness in one eye. It is exhilarating for Yosief to express himself in this way.

Yosief spent a lengthy time in different hospitals, including a mental health hospital, and in rehabilitation centres. Considering that he had to be trained to learn the basics, like his name and date of birth, and being introduced to his offspring, the current status and situation are grossly amazing to him and those who followed him closely.

It is this great achievement that the book *Glance at Eternity* narrates. Whether you want to see it as a self-help and self-confidence-building story or you want to follow an amazing story, the book claimed above is for you.

Further in this book, *Duplicitous Mindsets*, Yosief explores his new analytical skills in social and political scenarios. Yosief analyses the equation he came up with—*failure + excuse = blame.*

Duplicitous Mindsets explores the newly acquired analytical mind of the author, Yosief Tewolde. It is seen with amazement by people who knew Yosief, who claim he is living a second life.

One will find that the aim of the book is to raise questions in the readers' mind. It reflects to various circumstances stated shortly.

It looks into political and social analysis.